Ivan Lendl

By
Chip Eliot

Edited By
Michael E. Goodman

CRESTWOOD HOUSE
Mankato, Minnesota
U.S.A.

Eliot, Chip
  Ivan Lendl

  SUMMARY: A biography of tennis star Ivan Lendl, the number one player in men's tennis in 1986 and 1987.
  1. Lendl, Ivan, 1960- —Juvenile literature. 2. Tennis players-Czechoslovakia—Biography—Juvenile literature. [1. Lendl, Ivan, 1960- . 2. Tennis players.] I. Goodman, Michael E. II. Title. III. Series.
GV994.L36E55   1988   796.342'092'4—dc19   [B]   [92]   88-1829
ISBN 0-89686-380-8

          International Standard   **Library of Congress**
              Book Number: **Catalog Card Number:**
              0-89686-380-8   **88-1829**

PHOTO CREDITS

Cover: Focus West (Todd Friedman)
Sports Illustrated: (Tony Triolo) 24-25; (Craig Molenhouse) 32-33, 45, 46; (Joe McNally) 38-39
Focus West: (Will Hart) 4, 12-13, 17, 28-29, 35; (Stewart Kendall) 7, 26, 36; (Mitch Reibel) 11;
    (Todd Friedman) 14, 18, 23, 40
SIPA Sports/Focus West: 8; (Roland Garros) 20-21
Wide World Photos: 43

Produced by Carnival Enterprises.

CRESTWOOD HOUSE

TABLE
OF
CONTENTS

LENDL TAKES THE TITLE...AGAIN

It is September 1987. The place is the National Tennis Center in Flushing Meadow, New York. The event is the U.S. Open, one of the year's most important tennis tournaments. Ivan Lendl is there to defend his championship title. He has won twice before, in 1985 and 1986, but this time he will face his toughest foes.

In the quarterfinals, he plays John McEnroe, who won the Open in 1979, 1980, 1981, and 1984. McEnroe has not been winning the way he once did, but he still is a tough opponent. McEnroe blasts Lendl with scorching serves and forehand smashes, but Lendl is able to handle anything Mac sends his way. He is in total control. When McEnroe rushes the net, Lendl fires a forehand shot past him. Lendl can do no wrong. He beats Mac in three straight sets 6-3, 6-3, and 6-4.

The semifinals are next. Lendl must now face Jimmy Connors, the man who called Lendl a "chicken" seven years before. Connors has won the Open in 1974, 1976, 1978, 1982, and 1983. It is said that with their records, Connors and McEnroe practically own the U.S. Open.

The momentum, however, is clearly with Lendl. Connors has lost his previous 13 matches with Lendl. Lendl makes it number 14 as he beats Connors 6-4, 6-2, and 6-2.

It appears that Lendl is on the way to his third straight U.S. Open title. His final opponent is Sweden's Mats Wilander. No one really expects Wilander to beat Lendl. But then it is

Ivan Lendl lunges to return a forehand shot.

learned that Lendl has come down with a bad case of the flu. If it were a less important tournament, Lendl might consider dropping out. However, the chance to win the Open again is too big a prize to pass up.

Luckily, rain gives Lendl an extra day of rest. When Monday's match starts, it appears that the one day of rest hasn't been enough. The first set seems to last hours. Both players are known for their speed, but today, Wilander seems faster. He takes the first set 7-6, but Lendl bounces back quickly. He shuts out Wilander 6-0 in the second set, using hard forehand shots and beautiful backhands that fall just inside the lines. Wilander comes close in the third set, but Lendl beats him 7-6. In the final set, Lendl never loses his serve. After a long and grueling ten games, Lendl finally triumphs 6-4, winning the Open again. The match lasts 4 hours and 47 minutes, a record for the Open.

Despite the flu, Lendl played brilliantly. Had the match gone on any longer, however, Lendl feels he might have lost. "I almost ran out of juice in the last sets," he told a reporter. Still, throughout the Open, Lendl showed the same qualities that made him a champion and the No. 1 men's player — stamina, strength, and an intense desire to win.

For his troubles, Lendl took home $250,000 in prize money. His year-end winnings total more than $800,000. Once again, there is no doubt who is the world's No. 1 men's tennis player. It is Ivan Lendl.

Concentration is the name of the game.

PRACTICE MAKES PERFECT

Ivan Lendl (pronounced E-VON LEN-DLE) was born on March 7, 1960, in Ostrava, Czechoslovakia, an industrial city near the Polish border. He was an only child. His father, Jiri, was a lawyer. He also was a top tennis player in Czechoslovakia in his younger days. Ivan's mother, Olga, was also a tennis player. She was once ranked the No. 2 women's singles player in the country.

When he was three years old, Ivan began tagging along with his mother during her daily practice sessions. By his fourth birthday, Ivan had already picked up a wooden paddle and was hitting balls against a wall. Ivan's parents could see he had the makings of a good tennis player. They encouraged him and practiced with him frequently.

As a young boy, Ivan was quite athletic. When he wasn't hitting a tennis ball, he was playing basketball and soccer. But tennis was his first love. On most sunny afternoons Ivan could be found on the local tennis courts. He would play anyone at the courts. If no one was there, he practiced against the wall. But Ivan preferred real opponents. "I could not beat the wall," he once told a reporter. Even as a young boy, Ivan showed the intense desire to win that would mark his professional career many years later.

Czechoslovakia is a country where people love sports. In towns and cities people form sports clubs and organize competitions and tournaments. Ostrava had several tennis

One more tennis ball comes flying across the net!

clubs, and Ivan joined one. Although he never took formal lessons, he did get many pointers from Oldrich Lerch, an instructor at the club. He helped Ivan learn to "jump on the ball," to play aggressively.

At first, Lendl had a weak forehand stroke. With help from Lerch and his parents, Ivan worked and worked on his forehand. With more practice, he learned to hit the ball harder and more accurately. He also carefully observed other, more experienced players. He would study their moves and copy them. He would play a set whenever the opportunity arose, whether it was with an instructor, his parents, or even the club ballboys.

When he was eight, Ivan entered his first real tournament. It was a less than spectacular start. In the first round, he lost the first set 6-0. He won a game in the second set, but eventually lost 6-1. Ivan didn't make it past the opening round of the tournament, but he was determined to try again soon.

As he grew, Ivan gained strength in his arms and became faster. He kept entering tournaments and slowly began winning them. His forehand, once weak, was now a powerful weapon. He also learned to use "topspin." By hitting the ball a certain way, he could make it spin very fast. When it landed on the other side of the court, it would take odd, fast-hopping bounces. Ivan began to get a reputation as a player to watch in the coming years.

In his early tennis career, Ivan worked to improve his forehand.

Ivan skillfully hits a difficult backhand shot.

A TEENAGE TRAVELER

As a schoolboy, logic was Ivan's favorite subject. "It fascinated me," he said. "I don't like mysteries. I feel there is a reason for anything that happens."

That same logical attitude spread to Ivan's tennis game. He

saw how practice and tricks like topspin had helped his game. He kept observing other players, learning their strengths and weaknesses. He learned how to incorporate the strengths into his style. He also developed strategies to take advantage of his opponents' weaknesses.

As a teenager, Ivan started playing in major international

junior tennis tournaments. He was just 15 when he arrived in the United States for the first time in 1975. He entered a tennis tournament that took place at the Orange Bowl in Florida. He won enough matches to make it to the quarterfinals before being eliminated.

Ivan found America to be quite different from his homeland. As he later told a reporter, "Coming to the United States was a culture shock. The language, the technology, nothing was the same." Ivan spoke some English, but not much. As a result, he kept to himself and had little to say to reporters or his fellow players. Because of that, he got a reputation as a moody, tight-lipped, unfriendly person.

"I wasn't afraid of talking," he later explained to another sportswriter. "It was just that when I came here, I didn't know anything about the country. The cars were so big. The streets were so big. Everything was so big. And they were speaking a language I didn't understand very well. My only knowledge of America was from old Chicago gangster movies."

Ivan was as determined to learn English as he had been to learn tennis. He found that one of the best ways to work on his English was to watch TV shows. One of his favorites was *Happy Days.*

In 1976, Ivan made it to the final rounds of the Banana Bowl, a tennis tournament that took place in Brazil. He played well, but was beaten by another young, fast-rising tennis star, John McEnroe. It would not be the last time these two stars would battle it out for the top title at a tournament.

By age 17, Ivan had risen in the junior rankings to the No.

Keeping his eye on the ball.

1 spot. He had won the French and Italian juniors titles and had won an important championship match at the Orange Bowl. He was voted the Best Junior Tennis Player in the World in 1978. But the jewel in his crown was the Wimbledon juniors title. The Wimbledon tournament takes place each year in England and is perhaps the most famous tennis event in the world. By winning the juniors title there, Ivan had boosted himself to the top of the junior tennis world. He dreamed of someday winning the senior men's title at Wimbledon's Centre Court.

Despite his success, Ivan was growing restless in the junior division. He felt he needed the challenge of playing older and better players. "I should have stopped earlier," he would later tell an interviewer. "I was winning too easily in the juniors. I forgot that there were players who could beat me," he said.

GOING PRO

In 1979, Ivan decided to join the ranks of professional tennis players. That meant starting over in the rankings. While he had been No. 1 in the junior division, he began as No. 74 in the senior division, according to the computer rankings of the Association of Tennis Professionals.

In the summer of 1979, Ivan traveled to Paris for the French Open. One of the first opponents he faced was the American player, Arthur Ashe. Ashe, a veteran, was one of the ten best players in the world. Ivan surprised Ashe and the crowd by defeating him. At the end of the match, Ivan thrust his arms

When Ivan wins a match, he shows it!

up and joyfully leaped into the air. It was a great moment for Ivan. It marked the first time he had defeated a top ten player. Ivan couldn't wait for his next matches.

His excitement, however, was short-lived. Two days later, he was matched against another star player, Vitas Gerulaitis. Gerulaitis beat the young Czech in three straight sets. For every game Ivan won against Gerulaitis, Gerulaitis won three.

With a powerful leap, Ivan makes another shot.

Still, Ivan was very happy with his performance. Gerulaitis was a fast player who hit the ball very hard. Ivan had managed to win six games. Arthur Ashe was among the most experienced players in men's tennis, and Ivan had defeated him. Ivan felt that his victory over Ashe had shown the world that he, too, was now a world-class player. But his match with Gerulaitis had taught him an even more important lesson. He realized that he still had to work on his game and polish his skills if he was to reach the top ranks of the tennis world.

Later that year, Ivan knocked off another top ten player, Eddie Dibbs. By the end of 1979, he had racked up enough victories to boost himself into the top 20 in the computer rankings. His winning record also earned him another honor

— *Tennis* magazine's award for Rookie of the Year.

In 1980, Ivan entered 35 major tournaments and won seven of them. At that time, the No. 1 ranked player in the men's division was Sweden's Bjorn Borg. Borg was a superb athlete who had won at Wimbledon five years in a row from 1976 to 1980. Lendl met Borg at the Canadian Open. Using his now explosive forehand and tricky topspin strokes, Lendl surprised the tennis world by defeating Borg.

Ivan ended 1980 on another happy note. The Czechoslovakian team had never won the Davis Cup (the Davis Cup is a very famous competition between teams of different countries). Thanks to Ivan's great playing in 1980, the Czechs took home the prized Davis Cup for the first time.

"TANKING IT"

By early 1981, Ivan had risen to No. 6 in the world rankings. In January 1981, Ivan entered the Volvo Masters tournament in New York City's Madison Square Garden. The Masters was for the top-ranked players only, and the tennis world was eager to see matches between Jimmy Connors, John McEnroe, Bjorn Borg, Ivan Lendl, and others.

In the third round, Ivan played against Connors. The match between Connors and Lendl would determine the opponents they would face in the fourth round. The winner of the match would undoubtedly face Bjorn Borg, who seemed almost unbeatable at the time. The loser would face a lower-ranked and easier opponent, Gene Mayer.

His forehand improved, and in 1979 Ivan was named Rookie of the Year.

Ivan gave Connors a hard fight in the first set but then seemed to lose his desire to win. He played badly and lost. To many, including Connors, it seemed as if Ivan had deliberately lost the match. By beating Mayer, Ivan would get into the finals and finish second overall. Finishing second in the tournament, he would earn $35,000 more than a third-place finish.

As expected, Connors was defeated by Borg, insuring that Connors would finish in third place. Connors was furious. He publicly called Ivan a "chicken." He accused him of "tanking it," or losing deliberately in order to win more money and face an easier opponent.

Ivan went on to face Borg in the finals. The sturdy Swede overpowered Ivan with blasts from the backcourt. Some rallies lasted more than 40 shots, and Ivan grew tired. His forehand stroke proved ineffective, and Borg won three straight sets, 6-4, 6-2, and 6-2.

The loss against Borg, the world's best men's player, was nothing to be ashamed of. However, Ivan came under heavy attack for his play in the Connors match. Connors had beaten Ivan in eight of their previous matches, but fans still expected Ivan to show his usual intense desire to win. At first, Ivan denied he had "tanked it." He said he was tired and not feeling very well. But a year later, he admitted that he had deliberately lost.

"I threw the second set away," he admitted. "Definitely, I did." However, Ivan explained that the tournament schedule had forced him to play two matches in two days, tiring him out.

Ivan smashes the ball across the net to his opponent.

Ivan (fourth from the right) is ready to try any new sport!

Why had he denied "tanking it"? he was asked. "I just wasn't ready to fight with the press," he answered, "because if I said, 'Okay, I tanked,' they would have said, 'you shouldn't do that,' and then I would hear about it all the time. I just wanted to get to bed early, so I changed my game in the second set and went."

Tennis fans were puzzled. Was Lendl "the toughest pro in tennis," as one magazine had said? Or was he a "chicken," as Jimmy Connors charged? The chicken label stuck for much of 1981. It would take more than a year for Ivan to finally shake it off.

DISAPPOINTMENTS AND VICTORIES

Six months after the Volvo Masters tournament, Ivan met Borg again in the finals of the French Open. Borg was unstoppable. Although it was a hard-fought battle, Borg finally dominated Ivan and beat him.

Ivan suffered another disappointment later that year. He was knocked out of the competition at Wimbledon in the very first round. To add insult to injury, he was defeated by an unknown Australian player, Charlie Fancutt.

Ivan hoped to end the year on a bright note by helping Czechoslovakia win its second Davis Cup. He got off to a good start, beating John McEnroe. Then the American doubles team triumphed over Ivan and his partner. Connors, still angry over Lendl's "tanking it," beat Lendl 7-5 and 6-4, ensuring victory for the U.S. team.

Despite the losses, Ivan quickly recovered his winning ways. At the start of 1982, John McEnroe was ranked No. 1 and Jimmy Connors was No. 2. Ivan would soon defeat them both and move into the No. 2 spot in the rankings.

Ivan was on a hot winning streak. He won matches at the WCT Gold Coast Classic in Florida and the Molson Tennis Challenge in Toronto, Canada. In the Molson match, he faced John McEnroe in the final round and won. Ivan racked up victory after victory. His winning streak reached 44 straight matches until Frenchman Yannick Noah defeated him in a California tournament. The 44-game winning streak was the

Ready for another backhand smash!

After a close call by the officials, Ivan disagrees with their decision.

second-longest one in open tennis history.

Ivan still could not gain the No. 1 ranking in men's tennis. He had won dozens of tournaments, but he had not won any Grand Slam events. The Grand Slam events are Wimbledon, the U.S. Open, the French Open, and the Australian Open. Until Lendl had managed to win one of them, he would not be considered the undisputed No. 1 player in the world.

THE TWO MILLION DOLLAR MAN

By the spring of 1982, Ivan was recognized as the steadiest and most consistent player in the men's division. Since the U.S. Open in 1981, he had lost only three matches.

Many tennis fans expected Ivan to win his first Grand Slam event at the 1982 French Open. He was seeded, or ranked, second in the tournament. But he could only make it to the fourth round before being knocked out of the tournament by an unseeded Swedish player, Mats Wilander. Wilander played well, matching Ivan's powerful shots from the baseline. Ivan's trusty forehand failed him. After the match, Ivan said, "My timing was off, especially in my forehand. That's why he was outplaying me from the baseline. I can't do much without my forehand."

Ivan was disappointed by the loss. His grueling non-stop schedule had also left him very tired. He decided to skip Wimbledon. His next tournament was the Canadian Open. He had won it twice before, in 1980 and 1981. This time, however, he was stopped by Vitas Gerulaitis.

A few weeks later, he beat Jimmy Connors in the semi-finals of the Association of Tennis Professionals (ATP) Championship. In the final round, Ivan defeated Steve Denton, adding another title to his list of victories.

Still, victory at a Grand Slam event eluded him. At the U.S. Open, he got off to a shaky start. His timing and forehand seemed off against his first round opponent. Tim Mayotte played well enough against Ivan in the second round to force the match to go to five long sets. The momentum now seemed to be with Ivan. He took matches from Mats Wilander and Kim Warwick. In the semifinals, he met John McEnroe again. This time, he demolished McEnroe in straight sets. Only Jimmy Connors stood in the way of the critical Grand Slam victory. Connors was also on a hot streak. He had beaten Ivan in eight of their last nine matches. Connors played brilliantly, returning Ivan's serves and smashes with ease. Ivan fell behind by two sets. He battled back to win the third set, but it wasn't enough. Connors took the fourth and final set, winning the U.S. Open for the fourth time.

Ivan got his revenge against Connors in January 1983. Ivan beat him easily at the Volvo Masters tournament, 6-3 and 6-1.

The 1983 Volvo Masters marked the official end of the 1982 tennis season. It had been a great year for Ivan. He'd won 15 major tournaments, tying a record set by Jimmy Connors and Guillermo Vilas. His prize money for 1982 had topped the $2 million level. That didn't even count all the money he made from commercial endorsements and appearances at tennis exhibition matches!

Ivan explains the finer points of a backhand shot to a group of Big Brothers and Big Sisters participants.

From his winnings, Ivan began collecting sports cars and bought a house for himself in Greenwich, Connecticut.

A GRAND SLAM VICTORY AT LAST

Ivan had always played well on indoor tennis courts. In early 1983 he had a 66-game winning streak. That streak was broken when he faced John McEnroe at the U.S. Pro Indoor Tennis Championship. McEnroe was eager to avenge his loss to Ivan at the Volvo Masters earlier in the year. He played aggressively, rushing the net and taking advantage when Ivan was forced to use a weaker second serve.

Ivan has a powerful first serve that has been clocked at speeds up to 140 miles per hour. Some experts say he hits the ball harder than any tennis player. But when Ivan faults (fails to get his first serve inbounds), and has to serve a second time, he is more cautious. In order to make sure his second serve is on target, he serves the ball more slowly. At the Volvo Masters, McEnroe took advantage of Ivan's slower second serve and smashed the ball back to keep Ivan off-balance. Ivan took the first set, but Mac roared back and took the next three to win.

Later in 1983, Ivan injured a triceps muscle in his upper arm. He was forced to miss many tournaments in the spring. By summer, he was healthy again and eager for Wimbledon. The courts at Wimbledon are grass, making them the fastest in the world, according to many people. The courts were

Preparing for another hard-driving, intense game.

Ugh! Ivan pushes himself for another shot.

better for serve-and-volley players like McEnroe. These players hit hard serves and rush to the net to volley the ball, or hit it back before it bounces. Ivan's strength was hitting long hard ground strokes from the backcourt, so he was at a disadvantage on the grass courts. Despite the surface, he made it into the semifinals. John McEnroe, playing near the peak of his form, defeated Ivan again.

Still, 1983 had been another good year for Ivan. He made it to the finals in 13 of the 22 tournaments he entered. He won 68 matches and lost only 15. He won the Seagram Seven Crowns of Sport award for Men's Tennis Player of the Year.

Ivan missed part of the 1984 season because of a pulled hamstring muscle in his thigh. By summer, however, he was ready for another rematch against John McEnroe at the French Open. Mac had won 42 matches in a row and was hot. Mac jumped to an early lead, taking the first two sets. But Ivan kept the pressure on and McEnroe began making mistakes. Ivan attacked with a variety of passing shots, lobs, and smashes until he tied the match. In the tiebreaker, he edged McEnroe 7-5 for his first Grand Slam Victory! Ivan hoped it would silence the critics who said he often choked under pressure.

But Ivan's joy was short-lived. Soon after the French Open, Connors beat him in the semifinals at Wimbledon. Then McEnroe had his revenge at the U.S. Open, defeating Ivan in the finals. Once again, critics said Ivan was the "championship loser," or the champ who couldn't win that big game.

After a long practice, Ivan still has time to play with his two dogs.

THE CHAMPION NO ONE CARES ABOUT

Throughout 1984 and 1985, Ivan continued to work on his game. He learned to adapt to grass courts and other hard-surfaced courts like those at Flushing Meadow. He worked hard to improve his second serve. He perfected a topspin stroke on his backhand. He also changed his personal habits. He gave up red meat, sweets, and starches. He ran long distances to build up his strength and stamina. He ran wind sprints to give him speed. His weight dropped from 185 to 170.

Ivan's training paid off. Boris Becker had won at Wimbledon in 1985. He was just 17, the youngest player to win that event. In early 1986, Ivan met the young West German at the Nabisco Masters and beat him in three sets. It was his 35th victory in 36 matches. He had won close to $2 million in 1985!

Throughout 1986, he kept winning matches. Yet he wasn't winning the hearts of tennis fans as Connors and McEnroe

Ivan's smooth form wins matches.

had once done. Off the court, Ivan seemed moody and unfriendly, with little to say to anyone. His cool attitude led some sportswriters to call him "The Grim Reaper," or "The Tin Man." Others said he was just boring.

Ivan defended himself by explaining that he was not completely comfortable living in America. His lack of confidence in his English led him simply to keep his mouth shut. He also said he was different from Jimmy Connors or John McEnroe. "If you want comedy or tantrums, don't look at me," he told a reporter. When *Sports Illustrated* put him on its cover in late 1986, the headline read "The Champion No One Cares About."

Throughout all this bad publicity, Ivan continued to work at improving his tennis. At his home in Greenwich, he practiced hard on his own tennis court. He wanted to make sure he was ready for the 1986 U.S. Open. Every time the courts at the National Tennis Center (home of the U.S. Open) are resurfaced, Ivan hires the same workers to resurface his own tennis court. He makes sure that his court and the court at the U.S. Open are in the exact condition.

As he played against Frenchman Henri Leconte in the 1986 U.S. Open, Ivan made a spectacular shot — he drove a hard forehand shot down the line which Leconte couldn't return. It was the best shot of the entire Open and fans finally had to stand up and cheer the Czech champ. Ivan went on to win the finals and take his second U.S. Open.

"The way to win fans," Ivan said later, "is by winning and winning and winning." That's exactly what Ivan Lendl was doing.

Taking time to "step out" in style.

NO. 1

In 1986 and 1987, Ivan was the undisputed No. 1 player in men's tennis. 1987 was a particularly good year for him.

He was at the peak of his power, and the newspaper headlines said it all. "Lendl Overpowers Jarryd," said one headline after Ivan won his seventh Grand Prix event of the year. "Lendl Prevails," the papers announced when he won the European Community Championships. "Lendl Defeats Leconte," "Becker Falls to Lendl," "Lendl Rips Wilander" were just a few of the 1987 sports headlines.

In his personal life, Ivan found it easier to relax now that he was universally acknowledged as No. 1. Off the courts, he found a lot more time to enjoy golf, his second favorite sport. Ivan enjoys golf so much that he has enthusiastically organized several charity golf tournaments. He even said that he sometimes rushes through practice or even matches to get onto the golf course for a game.

In December 1987, eight of the best men's tennis players met in the Nabisco Masters tournament in New York. The Nabisco Masters is considered by many to be the world championship of tennis. Brad Gilbert, Boris Becker, Stefan Edberg, Mats Wilander, Milo Mercir, Jimmy Connors, Pat Cash, and Ivan Lendl were all hoping to end the year with a big victory. Ivan met Gilbert in his first match. Gilbert had lost 13 previous matches with Lendl. In fact, he'd never beaten Lendl. This time was no different—Lendl trounced him 6-2, 6-2. Lendl barely broke a sweat, sportswriters noted, as he beat player after player to win the tournament. The victory solidified Lendl's grasp on the No. 1 ranking in men's tennis. It also, said one sportswriter, earned him the right to be mentioned with Connors, McEnroe, and Borg as one of the

Enjoying his second-favorite sport.

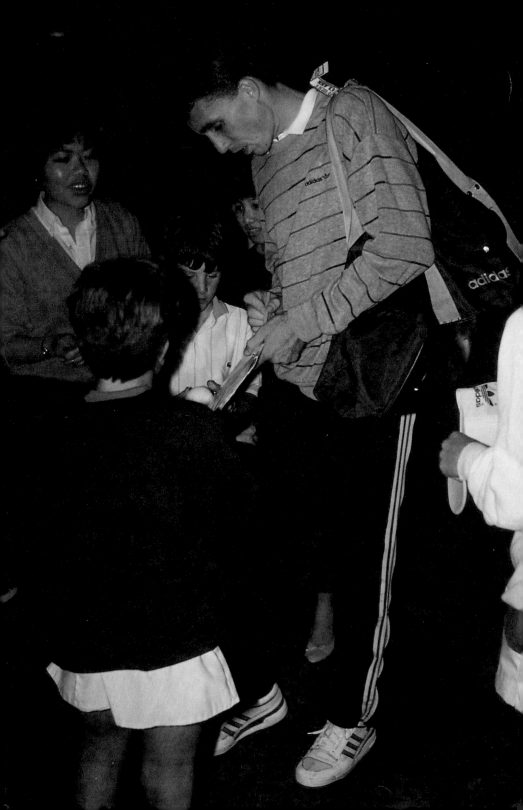

best tennis players of the modern era.

Ivan had been correct about winning fans by winning games. By year's end, tennis fans were cheering Ivan loudly at every appearance. When he was in a match, fans knew they could count on excitement and great tennis. Even the critics and writers had come to admire him. Again, a newspaper headline summed it up perfectly. "Win or Lose," the paper proclaimed, "Lendl Is a Hit."

Ivan is recognized throughout the tennis world as a No. 1 player.

IVAN LENDL'S PROFESSIONAL STATISTICS

Year	Wins	Losses	Winning Streak(s)	Titles Won	ATP* Rank
1980	109	28	19	7	6
1981	96	14	35, 44	10	2
1982	106	9	26	15	3
1983	75	16	10, 17	7	2
1984	62	16	11	3	3
1985	84	7	31, 29	11	1
1986	74	6	25	9	1
1987	74	7	25	8	1

*Association of Tennis Professionals